TABLE OF CONTENTS

Craig Phillips (b. 1961) is a native of Nashville, Tennessee. He holds the degrees Doctor of Musical Arts, Master of Music and the Performers Certificate from the Eastman School of Music. Rochester, New York, where he studied with the late Russell Saunders. He was winner of the First Prize in the 1994 Clarence Mader Competition for organ composition and was a finalist in the Mader National Organ-Playing Competition in 1991 and the Fort Wayne National Organ-Playing Competition in 1986. He maintains an active concert schedule and has appeared as soloist with members of the Eastman Philharmonia, the Oklahoma Symphony, the Los Angeles Mozart Orchestra and Musica Angelica at the Corona del Mar Baroque Festival.

Increasingly in demand as a composer, Dr. Phillips has received many commissions, including those from Washington National Cathedral, The Association of Anglican Musicians, University of California, Riverside, duo-organ team, The Chenaults, and Episcopal cathedrals in Buffalo, Portland and Atlanta. His works have received critical acclaim in journals such as *Clavier, The American Organist, Cross Accent,* and *The Journal of the Association of Anglican Musicians*. His compositions have been featured on National Public Radio's *Pipedreams*. He was the recipient of a 1993 Meet the Composer grant for a song cycle premiered at the Ojai Festival. His organ and choral works are published by a number of firms.

Dr. Phillips is Music Associate at All Saints Episcopal Church in Beverly Hills. With the semi-professional choir of that church he has made two East Coast tours and recorded for Gothic Records. He is a member of the American Guild of Organists, the Association of Anglican Musicians and the American Society of Composers, Authors and Publishers. Dr. Phillips is represented by The Young Organists Cooperative.

For Peter Fyfe

What Wondrous Love Is This

Wondrous Love

Sw. String Celeste 8'
Gt. Flute 8'; Sw. to Gt. 8'
Ped. 16' and 8'; Sw. to Ped. 8'

William Walker's *Southern Harmony*, 1843
Arranged by Craig Phillips

For Bob Beatty

Adagio

Sw. String Celeste 8'
Gt. Solo Flute 8'
Ped. 16' and 8'; Sw. to Ped.

CRAIG PHILLIPS

For Russell Saunders

Praise to the Lord, the Almighty

Lobe Den Herren

Sw. Full with Reeds
Gt. Full with Reeds; Sw. to Gt. 8'
Ped. 16', 8' and 4'; Sw. to Ped. 8'

Stralsund Gesangbuch, 1665
Arranged by Craig Phillips

For Sharron Lyon

Amazing Grace! How Sweet the Sound

Amazing Grace

Sw. String and Flute 8'
Gt. Full; Sw. and Ch. to Gt. 8'
Ch. String and Flute 8'; Sw. to Ch. 8'
Ped. Solo Reed 4'

Virginia Harmony, 1831
Arranged by Craig Phillips

*The 10th of the chords may be omitted or redistributed if the reach is too large.

For Helen Cantrell

O Come, O Come Emmanuel

Veni Emmanuel

Sw. String and Flute 8'
Gt. Principals 8', 4' and 2'; Reed 8'
Ch. Solo Reed 8'
Ped. 16' and 8'; Sw. to Ped. 8'

Plainsong
Arranged by Craig Phillips

20

Sw. Full with Reeds
Fast, driving (slightly detached)

For David Oliver

It Is Well With My Soul

Ville du Havre

Sw. String Celeste 8'; Flute 8'
Gt. Principal 8'; Sw. to Gt. 8'
Ped. 16' and 8'; Sw. to Ped. 8'

PHILIP P. BLISS
Arranged by Craig Phillips

For Jim Cochran

If You Will Only Let God Guide You

Neumark

Sw. String and Flute 8'
Ch. Reed 8'
Ped. 16' and 8'

GEORG NEUMARK
Arranged by Craig Phillips

for David Littler

Voluntary on "Lift High the Cross"

Crucifer

Sw. Full with Reeds
Gt. Plenum, Sw. coupled
Ped. Full with Reeds 16' and 8'

SYDNEY HUGO NICHOLSON
Arranged by Craig Phillips

*For my mother, Karen Neihart Phillips and Lynn M. David, Jr.
on the occasion of their wedding Christmas Eve, 1984*

Sw. Flute 8'
Gt. Reed 8'
Ped. 16' and 8'

Pastorale

CRAIG PHILLIPS

Calmly, but dancing

*On a three manual instrument the hands may be divided with a string sound in the left hand and a flute in the right.

Aria

Sw. String 8' and Flute 8'
Gt. Flute 8'; Sw. to Gt. 8'
Ped. 16' and 8'

CRAIG PHILLIPS

for Carol Foster

Savior of the Nations, Come

Nun komm, der Heiden Heiland

Sw. Cornet
Ch. Soft founds. 8'
Ped. Soft 16' and 8'

melody from *Erfurt Enchiridia*, 1524
Arranged by Craig Phillips

44

For Donna Whited

All Glory, Laud, and Honor

St. Theodulph

Sw. Solo Reed 8'
Gt. Principals 8', 4' and 2'; Mixture
Ped. Principals 16', 8' and 4'

MELCHIOR TESCHNER
Arranged by Craig Phillips